# SANTORINI

## TRAVEL GUIDE 2024

### Craft Your Perfect Greece Odyssey For An Unforgettable Mediterranean Escape

Friedrich C. Vincent

Copyright © Friedrich C. Vincent

All rights reserved.

No part of this publication may be reproduced, stored, or transmitted in any form or by any means, electronic, mechanical, photocopying, recording, scanning, or otherwise without written permission from the publisher. It is illegal to copy this book, post it to a website, or distribute it by any other means without permission.

First edition 2024

## ABOUT THE AUTHOR

Friedrich is a passionate traveler and adventurer who has explored some of the world's most beautiful and exotic destinations. He has always been fascinated by the different cultures, histories, and landscapes of the places he visits, and has made it his mission to discover the hidden gems of every location.

As a tourist, Friedrich believes that travel should be about more than just seeing the sights - it should be a journey of self-discovery, where you connect with the people and culture of the places you visit. He strives to create immersive travel experiences that allow him to truly understand and appreciate the local customs and traditions.

Friedrich's love for travel and adventure has led him to explore many countries across the globe, from the deserts of Morocco to the rainforests of Costa Rica. His curiosity and thirst for knowledge have inspired him to write travel guides and articles that offer a unique perspective on the destinations he has visited.

In his writing, Friedrich combines his personal experiences with his research to provide readers with comprehensive and insightful travel advice. He aims to help travelers get the most out of their journeys, providing them with tips and insights that they won't find in traditional guidebooks.

# TABLE OF CONTENTS

| | |
|---|---|
| **ABOUT THE AUTHOR** | 2 |
| **My Trip To Santorini** | 7 |
| **INTRODUCTION** | **12** |
|    Geological Origins | 12 |
|    Minoan Civilization | 13 |
|    Historical Transitions | 13 |
|    Venetian Rule | 14 |
|    Ottoman Occupation | 15 |
|    19th Century and Independence | 15 |
|    Modern Times | 16 |
|    Tourism Boom | 16 |
| **CHAPTER 1** | **20** |
|    Travel Tips and Etiquette | 20 |
|    Practical Information | 25 |
|       Vacation Packing List | 25 |
| **CHAPTER 2** | **29** |
|    Planning Your Trip | 30 |
|       What To Know Before Traveling To Santorini | 30 |
|       Best way to get there | 30 |
|       Visa | 31 |
|       Best Time to Visit | 31 |
|       Transportation | 32 |
|       Time zone | 32 |
|       Currency | 33 |
|       Local customs | 33 |

| | |
|---|---|
| **CHAPTER 3** | **36** |
| Accommodation Options | 36 |
| Top Attractions in Santorini | 42 |
| Best Beaches | 59 |
| **CHAPTER 4** | **62** |
| Best Restaurants | 62 |
| Best Time to Visit | 70 |
| The Cheapest Time To Travel | 75 |
| **CHAPTER 5** | **78** |
| Transportation Options | 78 |
| How to Navigate Santorini | 78 |
| **CHAPTER 6** | **88** |
| Greek Phrases for Visitors | 88 |
| Festivals And Events | 95 |
| **CHAPTER 7** | **100** |
| Cuisines To Try | 100 |
| Traditional Santorinian Cuisine | 100 |
| Gourmet Experiences | 107 |
| Events & Culinary Festivals | 108 |
| Well-known Cafes | 112 |
| **CHAPTER 8** | **118** |
| Shopping in Santorini | 118 |
| Top Shopping Destinations | 118 |
| What to Buy and Where to Shop? | 118 |
| **CHAPTER 9** | **128** |
| 5-day Trip Itinerary | 128 |
| DAY 1: Discovering Santorini's Magnificence | 128 |
| DAY 2: Leisure and Island Exploration | 129 |

    DAY 3: Tasting of Wine and Cultural Delights 130
    DAY 4: Island Exploration and Leisure    130
    DAY 5: Farewell    131

**CHAPTER 10**    **134**
  Traveling With Family or as a Couple    134
    Santorini as a Couple    134
    Best Location for Couples    137
    Top Activities for Couples    137
  Family-Friendly Activities    139

**CHAPTER 11**    **145**
  Emergency Contacts    145

**CONCLUSION**    **148**

## My Trip To Santorini

While Santorini is breathtakingly beautiful, the island's untamed nature is sometimes hidden. Although you can take a plane to the airport, I traveled to Ios as a student by ferry from Athens (yes, it may be tiring), which is known for being a party island. We took a few days off after we were all hung over. I would island-hop to enjoy everything that each island has to offer—some have water sports, others have incredible antiquities, and still others have breathtaking landscapes, cultures, and cuisine.

When we arrived at the port, there was a zigzagging path leading up to the main town. It was very steep and exhausting to walk in the heat, but if you are fit, you should try it. Arriving early in the morning or late in the afternoon is a great way to see the island, just be sure to look behind you. The vast and untamed splendor of the caldera is truly amazing. The attractive thing is that the buildings are all plainly whitewashed with some blue accents. Food is also delicious.

The archaeological sites are worth a visit, but there's not a lot to do there. In my opinion, I would stay on the island for a few days. If all you want is a fairly laid-back vacation, two weeks will do. In addition, there are other small cove beaches and an islet in the center of the Caldera that is somewhat volcanic.

I would try to visit the islands outside of the busiest travel seasons and utilize the ferries to bounce from island to island; they are all very different. We didn't make reservations for lodging; it's simple to arrive at the port of arrival; ladies, come down with a brochure if there are any rooms available; they are simple and clean. The meal was excellent.

# INTRODUCTION

It's official name, Thira, Santorini is a stunning gem in the Aegean Sea, noted for its crystalline waters, spectacular vistas, and the appeal of its white-washed villages perched on cliffs. Visitors become a part of a story that goes well beyond the present as they stroll through its winding lanes, discovering ancient ruins and enjoying the delicacies of Greek food. A tour through Santorini's rich and fabled past is necessary to fully understand the island.

## Geological Origins

Santorini's unique crescent shape and alluring magnetic pull are the result of a cataclysmic event that occurred during its geological formation. One of the biggest volcanic eruptions in recorded history took place about 3,600 years ago, creating the caldera that now defines Santorini. The Minoan eruption had a significant effect on the prehistoric societies of that era in addition to changing the island's landscape.

## Minoan Civilization

One of the most developed and vibrantly cultured societies of the Bronze Age, the Minoan civilization was based in Crete. Akrotiri's archeological site demonstrates Santorini's link to this civilization. Because of the volcanic ash that covered the city, Akrotiri has been preserved exceptionally well and provides a window into daily life during the height of the Minoan era.

Advanced plumbing systems, multi-story buildings, and elaborate frescoes depicting scenes of daily life, trade, and rites can all be found at Akrotiri. Excavations at the site have shown a society that was highly aware of art, architecture, and marine trade, highlighting Santorini's historical significance as a meeting point of ancient cultures.

## Historical Transitions

Over the ages, Santorini was ruled by several different people and cultures, such as the Mycenaeans, Dorians, and Byzantines. Due to its advantageous location in the

Aegean, the island was sought after by numerous civilizations, each of which left its cultural imprint on the island.

Santorini was an important center of Orthodox Christianity throughout the Byzantine era. Built monasteries and churches still stand as reminders of the island's spiritual past, decorated with elaborate murals and symbols. The island's history was further complicated during the Middle Ages when it was controlled by the Ottoman Empire and the Venetians.

## Venetian Rule

During the thirteenth century, Santorini was fortified with magnificent castles and towers by the Venetians, who realized the island's strategic significance. The architecture of Fira, the island's capital, combines ancient Cycladic architecture with medieval structures, a clear example of the Venetian influence. The ruins of castles, like the ancient fortress that was Skaros Castle in Imerovigli, bear witness to the legacy of Venetian sovereignty.

## Ottoman Occupation

In the sixteenth century, the Ottoman Empire took over Santorini, ushering in an era of trade and cultural interchange. The social structure of the island was influenced by the Ottomans, who brought aspects of their food, architecture, and way of life. The houses dotted about Santorini in the Ottoman architecture, especially in Pyrgos village, bear witness to the legacy of this era.

## 19th Century and Independence

As the island took part in the fight for Greek independence from Ottoman rule, Santorini saw substantial changes during this time. The islanders made significant contributions to the establishment of modern Greece in 1830 by taking part in the Greek War of Independence. After gaining independence, Santorini, like many other Greek islands, went through a phase of reconstruction and cultural revival.

## Modern Times

Santorini saw changes in the 20th century that would eventually make it a popular international tourist destination. Together with its rich history, the island's natural beauty drew visitors looking for sun-drenched scenery and a window into a colorful past.

Archaeological digs took off in the middle of the 20th century, providing fresh insights into the past civilizations of Santorini. The excavation of Akrotiri, which was started in the 1960s by archaeologist Spyridon Marinatos, yielded a wealth of artifacts and new information that cemented the island's reputation as an archeological wonder.

## Tourism Boom

In the second part of the 20th century, Santorini became a more popular destination for tourists from around the world. Greek postcards became well-known for their pictures of whitewashed houses set against turquoise backgrounds, which drew tourists from all over the world. With its breathtaking sunsets and quaint villages, the island's distinct charm drew in honeymooners, artists, and anyone else looking to escape to a timeless paradise.

The surge in tourism presented both chances and difficulties. In addition to fostering economic expansion, the flood of tourists made sustainable tourism practices necessary to protect Santorini's fragile ecological and rich cultural legacy. Maintaining the island's appeal as a travel destination has become dependent on efforts to find a balance between development and conservation.

Santorini in the present era: Santorini is a city that straddles the divide between its rich past and a contemporary, international identity. The island's classic architecture, which is distinguished by Cycladic design elements, never fails to enthrall tourists, while modern conveniences and opulent lodgings only serve to improve their trip.

With their winding lanes, colorful bougainvillea, and expansive vistas that beckon investigation, Oia, Fira, and Imerovigli continue to stand as living examples of

Santorini's historical development. Santorini's history is not limited to the pages of textbooks but is viscerally present in the island's terrain thanks to its historical monuments, which include Akrotiri and Ancient Thera.

# CHAPTER 1

## Travel Tips and Etiquette

It's essential to be knowledgeable about travel etiquette and tips if you want to get the most out of your time on this charming Greek island.

**Recognizing Local Culture**

- Honoring Traditions

Santorini has a rich cultural past, and its residents are proud of its customs. Participating in regional customs, such as visiting festivals, sampling regional cuisine, or taking part in festivities, demonstrates respect

- Dress Modestly at Religious Sites

You must wear modest clothing when you visit churches or monasteries. Make sure you cover your knees and shoulders out of respect for these sites' religious significance.

## Navigating Transportation

- Renting a Car

Although Santorini's public transportation system is dependable, having a car, scooter, or ATV rental can provide you greater freedom to discover the island's lesser-known attractions. Make sure you have the required paperwork and abide by the traffic laws in your area.

- Public Transportation Etiquette

Be considerate of other passengers if you choose to take a bus or taxi. Give way to senior citizens for a seat, and exercise patience when driving on the island's narrow roads.

## Choosing Accommodation

- Reserve Early, Especially During the Busiest Time of Year, Destinations like Santorini are in high demand, especially during the summer. If you intend to go during the busiest travel season,

make your reservations early in advance to guarantee the greatest lodging at fair rates.
- Consider Staying in Classic Villages: If you want to fully experience Santorini, think about booking a room in a classic village like Oia or Fira. These places have serene ambiance, lovely architecture, and stunning vistas.

**Navigating Popular Sites**

- Arrive early to avoid the crowds and capture the famous Santorini sunset. Securing your location in advance is essential because popular spots like Oia can get congested as nighttime approaches.
- Go Beyond the Well-Known Places, Santorini has undiscovered treasures just waiting to be found, even if Oia and Fira are must-see locations. For a more personal encounter, veer off the beaten route and discover hidden beaches and lesser-known towns.

**Dining Ettiquette**

- Sample the Local Food: Greek food is very good in Santorini. Sample some of the regional specialties, such as moussaka, souvlaki, and fava, to fully experience the flavors. Given that Santorini is known for its vineyards, don't forget to complement your dinner with regional wines.
- Respect Meal Times: Greek dinners typically start later in the evening and are larger in scope. Take note of the local dining hours and savor the relaxed atmosphere during meals. In Santorini, it is not customary to rush through supper.

**Interaction with Locals**

- Learn Foundational Greek Phrases: Even though most people in Santorini understand English, striking up a conversation with a few simple Greek words might help a lot. Visitors that attempt to speak with locals in their language are greatly appreciated.

- Be Patient and Polite: Friendliness and politeness are highly valued by Greeks. In your encounters, be kind and patient, particularly when things are hectic. Talk to people in the area to learn more about their culture and way of life.

**Respecting the Environment**

- Sustainable Tourism Practices

Santorini's natural beauty is a treasure worth preserving. Practice sustainable tourism by disposing of waste responsibly, participating in eco-friendly activities, and respecting nature while exploring the island.

- Water Conservation

Water scarcity is a concern on the island, so use water judiciously. Conserve water when possible, and opt for eco-friendly activities that minimize environmental impact.

**Navigating the Climate**

- Stay Hydrated

Santorini's climate can be hot, especially during the summer months. Stay hydrated by carrying a reusable water bottle, and take breaks in the shade to avoid heat exhaustion.

- Sun Protection:

Protect yourself from the intense Greek sun by applying sunscreen regularly, wearing sunglasses, and using a wide-brimmed hat. Sun safety is crucial, especially if you plan on spending time outdoors.

## Practical Information

### Vacation Packing List

Before it comes to packing, there is a lot to consider before heading to the stunning island of Santorini.

This charming Greek location calls for a combination of fashionable attire and necessary items.

**Clothing**

Because of the Mediterranean temperature in Santorini, bring light, breathable clothing. Include items like

- Airy dresses and skirts for hot weather
- Swimsuits for beach excursions
- Cozy shorts and tee shirts
- Light jackets or sweaters for chilly evenings
- Robust walking shoes for touring

**Sun Protection**

Sun protection is essential because the Greek sun may be very strong.

- Broad-brimmed hat or fashionable cap
- Sunglasses with UV protection
- High SPF sunscreen
- After-sun cream to soothe sun-kissed skin

**Travel Essentials**

Remember the useful things that can help your trip go more smoothly:

- Travel insurance
- A valid passport, travel documents,
- Electronic device
- A lightweight daypack for excursions
- A portable phone charger

**Beach Accessories**

Santorini is well-known for its stunning beaches, make sure to pack appropriately.

- Beach towel
- Comfortable sandals or flip-flops
- Snorkeling equipment if you want to explore underwater

**Camera and Electronics**

Use the appropriate technology to capture amazing scenes and memories.

- Waterproof phone case
- Power bank for long trips
- Good camera

**Toiletries**

Maintain your hygiene regimen with these necessities:

- A basic first aid kit
- Travel-sized body wash, shampoo, and conditioner
- Toothbrush and toothpaste
- Deodorant

**Stylish Accessories**

Santarini's distinct appeal provides the ideal setting for stylish accessories.

- Statement jewelry
- Trendy sunglasses
- Trendy scarves or shawls for cooler evenings
- Elegant hat

**Cash and Credit Cards**

Make sure you can easily access cash while you're visiting the island.

- Enough cash for minor transactions
- Credit/debit cards
- A travel wallet or money belt for extra protection

**Light Reading Material**

Nothing beats relaxing on the beach or a quiet evening with a nice book or e-reader:

- Fiction or travel books
- Santorini reference book for additional information

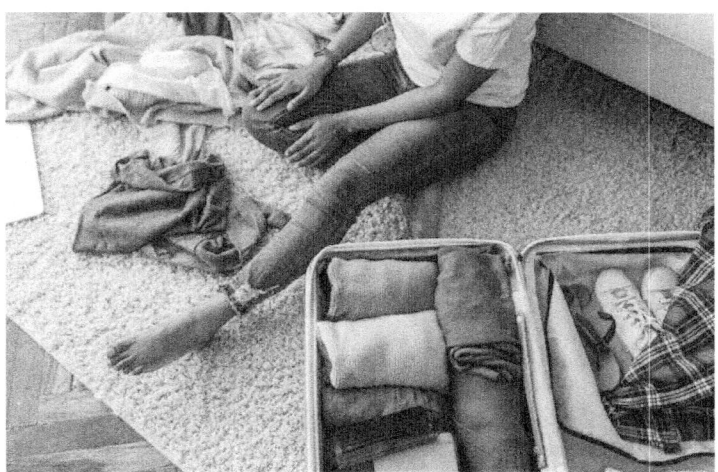

# CHAPTER 2

## Planning Your Trip

### What To Know Before Traveling To Santorini

### Best way to get there

- Flying

During the busiest travel seasons, seasonal direct flights from several European locations arrive at Santorini (Thira) International Airport. Most long-haul flights stop at Athens for a connection. From the airport, shuttles and taxis operate to the towns and resorts on the island.

- Ferries

Regular ferries arrive at Athinios ferry port near Fira after departing from Piraeus ferry port near Athens. Additionally, Santorini is connected by ferry to Mykonos and other Greek islands.

## Visa

Along with many other European nations, Greece is a member of the Schengen Area. Accordingly, visitors from specific nations are exempt from needing a visa for stays under ninety days, provided their passports will still be valid six months after the date of departure.

## Best Time to Visit

June to August is summer: Summer is the busiest season in Santorini, with many music and cultural events taking place. Low 80°F (high 20°C) average highs during this time of year are perfect for swimming, tanning, and exploring nearby islands.

However, May or September/October is a great time to visit to avoid the crowds and take advantage of significantly cheaper tour and lodging costs. During these months, temperatures can still reach 77°F (25°C).

## Transportation

- Car

The easiest way to get around is to rent a car, which can be done at the airport and large hotels.

- Bus

Buses run by KTEL connect the major towns of Fira, Oia, Perissa, and Kamari; however, there is no public transportation available to smaller towns or beaches.

- Taxis

You can get a taxi in Fira that will transport you almost wherever on the island. There are no ridesharing options accessible, like Uber.

## Time zone

Eastern European Standard Time.

Voltage/Plug Types : 230V and 50Hz are the standard voltage and frequency, respectively. Two spherical pins are on the plug.

## Currency

The European Union.

ATMs easily accessible

Are credit cards accepted everywhere?

Yes, except in smaller stores and cafés. It's still a good idea to have some cash on hand.

## Local customs

**Alcohol:** 18 years is the legal age in the federal government to purchase and consume alcohol.

**Water:** While you can use Santorini tap water for teeth brushing and washing, drinking it is not advised; instead, use bottled water.

**Public transportation:** Don't take up more than one seat, let others get off the boat before you board, and stand up to offer a seat to a pregnant woman or a person with a disability.

**Try using the language for communication:** As a show of respect, pick up a few simple phrases. For your convenience and comfort, locals will frequently switch to English, but they appreciate the effort

# CHAPTER 3

## Accommodation Options

There is a wide variety of lodging available in Santorini to suit different tastes and price ranges. With their opulent cliffside resorts offering breathtaking 360-degree views of the Aegean Sea and their little boutique hotels nestled in the center of Fira,

- Remezzo Villas

Excellent studio featuring large rooms, seclusion, and breathtaking views. Travel planning is aided by friendly staff. A four-course breakfast to remember. Pool and honeymoon suites have breathtaking views of the caldera.

- Dream Island Hotel

Lovely pool area with sea views and enough seating; the hotel in Thira offers a tranquil setting near the town center, shops, and bus station, pristine rooms and attentive staff; handy transportation options are available.

- Porto Fira Suites

Features large, contemporary accommodations, some with hot tubs, with breathtaking views of the caldera and sunsets. Great breakfast options, individual balcony, and friendly service. A bar area and pool provide relaxation.

- Hotel De Sol Spa

A classy hotel with a gorgeous pool, mouthwatering breakfast, and amazing architecture. Great personnel, a charming atmosphere, and a convenient shuttle service to Fira.

- Andronis Luxury Suites

Beautiful hotel including views of the caldera, infinity pools, gourmet breakfast, hot tubs in each room, wine choices, and a romantic ambiance.

- Above Blue Suites

Wonderful hotel with a separate terrace for eating and a great breakfast that is very varied. opulent apartments with their heated pools, hot tubs, and breathtaking views. great site.

- Pegasus Suites & Spa

Magnificent views of the caldera and the sunset, large rooms featuring terraces and plunge pools. Wonderful breakfast, suitable for a honeymoon. Options for a private pool and hot tub.

- Esperas Oia Santorini

Perfect cliffside setting with breathtaking views of the setting sun, a calm ambiance, private balconies, a restaurant, a swimming pool, and romantic possibilities. A lovely seaside location with unique cave chambers.

- Keti Hotel

A highly-rated hotel featuring spacious accommodations, amazing views of the caldera, and excellent hospitality.

features spacious bathrooms, private balconies, and top-notch amenities. An excellent setting for a romantic retreat.

- Heliotopos Hotel

little motel with a handmade breakfast, lovely views of the caldera, and kind staff. Cozy beds may be found in the rooms, and some have kitchenettes. On-site wine bar with a sunset view.

- Ducato di Oia

Aegean Sea vistas, stunning island views, and a central position in Oia. Perfect service, spotless accommodations with individual appeal, and individual swimming pools. Superb concierge assistance.

- You and Me Suites

Superior rooms featuring hot tubs, private pools, and sunset views. rooms with lovely décor and ample space. Free breakfast, excellent position, and breathtaking views of the caldera.

- Amaya Selection of Villas

Villas offer breathtaking views of the caldera, immaculately clean. Large, fully furnished rooms with personal hot springs and swimming pools. Ideal setting for exploring the neighboring stores and eateries and enjoying the sunset.

- Aria Suites

Excellent value, luxurious accommodations, breathtaking views, and spotless rooms. Large suites, free bubbly, and close access to dining establishments. a peaceful and enjoyable visit.

- Hill Suites

luxurious suites with breathtaking views in a lovely setting. Rooms are large and tastefully furnished, with individual hot tubs. Excellent service; eateries and stores are easily accessible on foot.

- Panorama Boutique Hotel

Magnificent views of the sea and caldera from the pool area, rooms, and balconies. Excellent food options, a staff that is welcoming, and a central location. Nicely furnished accommodations with a lovely poolside area.

- Oia Mare Villas

Beautiful setting atop a cliff, with amazing views of the sunset. Ideally located near stores, eateries, and Amoudi Bay, with a distinctive cave pool. Clean, tastefully appointed rooms, with porter service and transport close by.

- Anemomilos

Beautiful hotel with a range of lodging options, first-rate customer service, and breathtaking views. The on-site restaurant, hot tub, and pool are among the amenities. handy location next to Oia and the bus station.

- Santorini's Kokkinos Villas

Excellent views of the Caldera and the Aegean Sea from a convenient location. Rooms are large and tastefully decorated; some have private hot tubs. Breakfast offerings are delicious, the staff is friendly, and utilities are close by.

## Top Attractions in Santorini

- **Walk around the village of Oia**

Greece's and the Greek islands' most photographed village is the ancient village of Oia. The most well-known location in Santorini to view the sunset and volcano is here. With its picture-perfect views of the surrounding terrain, Oia is one of the caldera's most picturesque locations. A maze of cubic-shaped homes, whitewashed terraces, windmills, blue domes, and other marvels can be found there.

What to do: Savor the Sunset from Oia Kastro and Capture Images of the Windmill and Blue Dome Churches . Visit Ammoudi Harbor for lunch;

- **Go see the volcano, a dozing behemoth**

Santorini and other islands in the Aegean have been formed, destroyed, and reshaped by the active volcano. It destroyed the Minoan civilization in antiquity. The only way to reach the volcano, which is situated on "Nea Kameni," an islet facing the caldera, is via boat cruise. Once there, guests have the exceptional chance to explore a desolate area that is primarily adorned with black and red lava stones. From there, one can see the largest caldera in the world, together with the well-known whitewashed towns perched atop it. The hot springs are a must-see! There are hot springs close to the crater where you can swim because of the volcano's high temperatures. Situated on the deserted islet of Palea Kameni are the hot springs. Up to 35°C is reached in the water. The reddish-brown fluids known as sulfur waters are the product of volcanic activity.

The only way to get to the springs is by boat journey and tour. You can make use of their healing qualities while swimming.

- **View the volcanic crater or caldera**

The entire western side of the island is covered by Santorini's crescent-shaped caldera. One of the most breathtaking views of the volcano and the sea is provided by the tall volcanic cliffs. On the island, Oia, Fira, Imerovigli, and the other caldera communities are perhaps the most popular tourist destinations. In addition to the scenery, the distinct atmosphere draws a lot of visitors.

What to do: Some of the most exciting hiking paths in the Cyclades may be found close to the caldera's edge.

- **Swim on beaches with red and black sand**

Santorini's beaches differ greatly from those of other Cycladic islands, despite the island being a part of the Cyclades. Due to previous volcanic activity, Santorini has a special kind of beach with red and black pebbles or sand. That landscape creates the ideal contrast with the turquoise, crystal-clear waves of the sea!

- **Set out on an island-wide boat excursion**

The greatest thing to do is take a boat tour around Santorini. That kind of travel is quite well-liked. It gives you the chance to see the caldera from a different angle and to see the volcano, hot springs, and Thirasia Island.

Boat Daily Trips

Every day at various times, several tours are suggested. The best schedule is in the afternoon because you can watch the sunset. The excursion first takes you to Nea Kameni Island. You can stroll atop the active volcano and even make it to the crater's pinnacle there. You will next be taken to swim in the hot springs on the islet of Palea Kameni. A few tours also visit the island of Thirasia, which is located just in front of Santorini. The cost includes both the onboard meal and hotel pickup. Because this is the most visited site in Santorini, make reservations for your tour in advance!

- **A lavish Catamaran voyage**

A deluxe version of the boat trips is also offered, this time aboard an opulent catamaran. Snorkeling equipment, transportation from your hotel, and onboard food and drinks are all included in the full-day cruise. Additionally, you will experience the sunset distinctively after the day. Only small groups are permitted on luxury vacations, so there will be greater seclusion and peace of mind. There's food available as well, with generous servings of delectable barbecue. There is also an open bar. Note: Reserve your spot for the tour in advance as spaces are limited! The excursion is also available as a private tour or in a version at sunset.

- **Drive your vehicle and explore the island**

In addition to saving you time, renting a car in Santorini allows you to see locations that are difficult to get to by bus or day trip. Your trip to Santorini will go much more smoothly if you have your car. You'll have the freedom to explore at your speed and find less-known, hidden locations.

Finally, if you want to spend the majority of your time in a caldera hamlet, you might choose to rent a car for a brief amount of time to explore particular areas you are interested in seeing.

- **Explore the culinary scene**

Santorini's constantly developing food scene has elevated the island to the top of Greece's culinary traveler's list. The most well-known eateries include both exquisite food and breathtaking views of the sea. Several taverns are prepared to provide a genuine culinary experience at the same time.

Neighborhood Tavernas:Those little family-run eateries hold the key to authentic Greek cuisine. You may obtain great homemade traditional Greek meals at reasonable pricing by going to one. Psaraki and Metaxy Mas, two of the top taverns on the island, are among the best possibilities. There, you may sample traditional Greek cuisine in a traditional atmosphere.

Fine-dining Restaurants:Consider dining at Selene if you're craving an unmatched gourmet dining experience. It has embarked on a 35-year mission to embrace local ingredients and create a distinctive culinary environment, and it can easily be compared to the best restaurants in Europe.

- **Cooking class led by a local**

Are you looking to explore a more genuine side of Santorini and stray from the typical tourist route? You are welcome to schedule a cooking lesson with a nearby chef. In addition to enjoying a wine tasting, you will get the opportunity to learn how to cook Greek cuisine and prepare your farm-to-table dinner.

- **Enjoy regional wines while on a wine tour**

Every wine enthusiast should include Santorini on their travel bucket list. The soil's volcanic composition and the weather are the keys to success. In actuality, the island produces some of the best and most well-known wines in the entire world.

Since ancient times, wine has had a significant impact on the local economy and culture. It is merely one of the many reasons to adore Santorini these days. You can take part in a scheduled tour or explore certain wineries on your own.

- **Engage in jet ski excursions**

A jet ski safari is a unique way to explore the beaches on the southern coast of Santorini, and it's highly recommended for an unforgettable experience. You may reach those beaches by taking the "south coast tour". Some can only be reached by sea. Due to its popularity, the jet ski safari tour has limited availability. It's best to make reservations in advance!

- **Hiking from Oia to Fira**

Fira to Oia walk via Firostefani and Imerovigli towns is one of Greece's most beautiful island trekking paths. The volcanic caldera is traversed by the Oia trek in half. This three to four-hour session is highly recommended, even for novice hikers!

There are amazing views along the entire hiking path, which is thought to be very straightforward. To escape the scorching noon sun, it is advised to begin at dawn or before twilight. Although you can hike alone, it is advised that you follow a professional.

- **See other caldera villages**

Don't miss several more well-known settlements situated atop the caldera, which provide breathtaking views of the volcano and sunsets!

Fira

Santorini's capital city is the bustling hamlet of Fira. It's the perfect spot to see the sea, the volcano, and the traditional buildings of Santorini, which are perched above the sheer cliffs that form the caldera. The town also has a wide variety of stores and amenities. Numerous eateries and bars with breathtaking views may be found. Certain nightclubs are also lively till the wee hours of the morning. Take a stroll through the village, snap pictures of the blue-domed churches,

Visit the Archaeological Museum and Museum of Prehistoric Thera, have dinner while watching the sunset, and sip cocktails while taking in the views of the volcano. As you meander through Fira, don't forget to pay a visit to Firostefani, a nearby village a short distance north. There is the iconic installation of a caique (traditional fishing boat) on top of a terrace, which is part of the Homeric Poem hotel. Nearby is the charming "instagramic" Galini Cafe.

Imerovigli, the charming and romantic town

Another location to see the volcanic landscape of Santorini is Imerovigli, sometimes referred to as "the balcony to the Aegean." Couples especially like visiting the village in the golden hour. The best view of the volcano is provided by it. Walk to Theoskepasti Chapel and Skaros Rock; see Agios Ioannis Chapel, take pictures of the Blue-domed Church

- **Visit Ammoudi's small harbor**

Ammoudi is a little fishing harbor located directly beneath the hill from the well-known Oia hamlet. It's small but charming, with pubs serving up fresh seafood and fish that tastes great. Amoudi Bay does not have a beach, however some people swim there. A ten-minute stroll along the coast will bring you to the islet of Agios Nikolaos. You will see a lot of people swimming in the sea there. From the rocks, you can enter the water. Amoudi Bay is regarded as a stunning and serene location for sunsets.

- **Greece's Pompeii, Akrotiri**

Visit the ruins of the Akrotiri Minoan site, which date back thousands of years, to get an insight into Santorini's past. Indeed, the village is thought to have been built circa 4,500 B.C. It was approximately 1,650 B.C. when the volcano erupted, burying the old city beneath the earth.

- **Go to Cine Kamari to see a movie.**

The outdoor movie theater in Kamari Village is a highly well-liked summertime family pastime. The beautiful courtyard of Cine Kamari is home to a bar that offers beer, wine from the area, cocktails, and nibbles. Every day, there are two screenings. The movies are in Greek with English subtitles. Recognized as one of the world's top outdoor movie theaters, Cine Kamari has won awards. It is undoubtedly a different way to spend a true summer night in Santorini beneath the sky. Don't forget to include it on your schedule!

- **Transfers & tours by helicopter**

A popular luxury activity and recent trend in Santorini is helicopter tours and transfers.

 Helicopter excursions

Unforgettable views of the volcano, the volcanic island, and the caldera are available on a helicopter trip! Even while this new trend isn't the greenest method to see the island, it will nonetheless be an amazing experience!

Very few are available! Reservations must be made in advance.

Helicopter transportation between Santorini and Mykonos

A private helicopter transfer between Mykonos and Santorini is another option if you'd like to experience an opulent journey over the Aegean Sea! Traveling between islands in a quick, enjoyable, and secure manner is possible with private helicopter transports. They also provide you the chance to take in an unparalleled panoramic perspective of the Cycladic environment. You will see many of the most breathtaking locations on the islands throughout your transfer. This contains the well-known volcano of Santorini, striking cliffs, and charming whitewashed villages. Undoubtedly an experience of a lifetime

- **Participate in alternate tours and events**

Travelers visiting Santorini are starting to favor alternative tours more and more.

Photography Tours

With the help of these tours, you may view one of the world's most picturesque locations via the lens of a skilled photographer. In Santorini, photography tours are a popular trend that many young people are eager to sign up for! You will be able to photograph uncommon and infrequent locations with those tours. Furthermore, expert photographs of you with the most breathtaking backdrop will be captured.

Sea Kayaking

Sea Kayak Excursions are an exciting alternative activity that takes place on the southern shore. There are two trips available each day, one in the morning and one in the evening, that are ideal for families, friends, and couples. Additionally included in the program are swimming and snorkeling. Due to limited capacity, make your reservation in advance!

Tours by Fishing Boat

The traditional fishing boat tour is one of the activities that is more in line with the island's true way of life. Take a "caique" (a traditional wooden fishing boat) out fishing with the locals for a truly amazing supper. As the catch of the day is prepared and served for lunch or dinner, you will master various fishing techniques. all of this while taking in Santorini's breathtaking beach scenery and gorgeous sunset.

- **Explore traditional and medieval settlements**

Visit some of Santorini's traditional villages to see the island's real side! Situated off the beaten path, those charming communities on Santorini's mainland have managed to hold onto their original charm.

The medieval village of Emporia

With a strong medieval feel, Emporia is one of the most picturesque villages. A large number of refurbished stone mansions are now boutique hotels. You'll come across some intriguing architectural details as you meander around the alleys. The monuments and houses feature little balconies that are nearly joined to one another, as well as ancient, steep steps. In addition, they include arches and colorfully painted doorways. Pergola vines and bougainvillea trees add a touch of nature.

The former capital, Pyrgos

Since Pyrgos was formerly the capital of the island, it should also be on your list of places to visit. Situated on the flank of Mount Profitis Ilias is the settlement. Vineyards that yield the well-known Assyrtiko wine encircle it. Pyrgos maintains the cadence of island life while removing itself from the bustling Caldera tourist area. Its architectural features include whitewashed homes, medieval churches, and paved streets; the castle known as "Kasteli" is the main landmark.

The traditional village of Megalochori

Megalochori, with its numerous paved streets and alleyways, is another undiscovered gem. There, local architecture is prominently displayed. Megalochori is distinguished by its neoclassical palaces, blue domes, and elegant bell towers, among other features. There are also some fantastic neighborhood taverns throughout the village.

- **Explore Thirassia Island**

It is advised to incorporate a day trip to Thirassia if your stay in Santorini extends beyond four days. A tiny islet called Thirasia is situated very near to Santorini. It was separated from the rest of Santorini during a volcanic eruption. Only 319 people live there now, and mass tourism hasn't touched it. Thirasia and Santorini are similar twins. Though their personalities are vastly different, they share the same viewpoints, geology, and landscapes. Santorini is a vibrant island with state-of-the-art tourism facilities. Conversely, Thirassia keeps a low profile by continuing to live a traditional lifestyle. There are numerous scheduled boat cruises as well as a local ferry that leaves from the port of Ammoudi in Oia to get there.

## Best Beaches

The following beaches should be on your bucket list:

- **Red Beach**

This is the island's most striking beach. Given its name based on the hue of the rocks and sand, it presents an amazing sight! There is no organization at the beach.

- **Perivolos Beach**

One of the island's longest beaches, it is covered in shingle and black sand. Its volcanic terrain is incredibly fascinating, and its waters are pure and transparent! It's well-run, with rental sun lounges and other visitor amenities. In actuality, it is located in the famous Perissa beach's continuation.

- **Kamari Beach**

is well-known for its distinctive volcanic landscape. The beach is roughly 5 km long and has dark grey sand all across it.

Sun loungers and sun umbrellas are available at beach bars, hotels, restaurants, and other establishments along the shoreline.

# CHAPTER 4

## Best Restaurants

Top-notch restaurants have been built as a result of the millions of tourists that come to Santorini, particularly along the caldera where patrons may enjoy the distinctive scenery while dining. Although Greek and Mediterranean food dominates the culinary landscape, other cuisines are also present.

- **Selene**

Mediterranean

Selene Restaurant in Fira has been fusing local cuisine with culture for more than 30 years, so you can be sure that your meal will be the talk of your trip to Santorini. You will find many intriguing appetizers, main meals, desserts, and wines on its exquisitely designed menu.

- **Lycabettus**

Mediterranean

One of the best options for a romantic lunch or dinner in Santorini is the Lycabettus Restaurant, Enjoy some of the most delicious dishes from Santorini's fine dining scene on the balcony, accompanied by superb wine and a breathtaking view of the Aegean Sea and caldera.

- 1800 Floga

Oia

"1800" is a "living museum" that transports you to the previous century's atmosphere nowadays. It provides you with all the warmth and comfort of today, both within and out on the roof garden with its breathtaking sea view.

- **Mr. E**

Perivolos

Mediterranean

The contemporary eatery Mr. E is a great choice for upscale dining close to Perivolos. For every guest to have a distinctive culinary experience, The menu blends modern gastronomy with aspects of Cycladic cuisine. It is located at the Istoria Hotel.

- **Roka**

Oia

Mediterranean

Greek clay artists deliver delicious Greek food prepared with ingredients sourced from all around the country, paired with exceptional Greek wines, and served in ceramic creations. Good value for money, simplicity, a cozy atmosphere, and courteous service.

- **Lefkes**

Discover the flavors of Santorini at Lefkes restaurant, which is situated in Finikia in a traditional Santorinian home with a cozy ambiance. Its creative recipes are produced using top-notch ingredients and are inspired by Mediterranean cuisine.

- **Varoulko**

Varoulko is a terrific place to enjoy a delicious supper while taking in the breathtaking views of the sea, the caldera, and the volcano. It is located in one of Santorini's best sites. Wonderful full-course meals prepared by renowned chef Lefteris Lazarou and provided by helpful staff

- **Kapari**

Fira

The Kapari Restaurant can be found on the Fira major road, which is also the route that leads to Firostefani. The main focus of Dora and Costas, the husband and wife pair who own Kapari, has been meticulous attention to detail, and they have done a great job creating a lovely atmosphere inside.

- **Aroma Avlis**

In the town of Exo Gonia, Aroma Avlis is a Mediterranean restaurant located within Artemis

Karamolegos Winery. A variety of Greek wines are served, and many delectable dishes are prepared using traditional ingredients from Santorini, the Cyclades, and other parts of Greece.

- **Mataxi Mas**

Sometimes known as "in between us" in English, is a classic Greek tavern in Exo Gonia, Santorini. This tavern will demonstrate to you the excellence of Greek cuisine. In addition to indigenous Santorini cuisine, the "Metaxi mas" tavern serves food from various...

- **Kapari restaurant**

You can enjoy amazing culinary delights at the charming Kapari Wine Restaurant in Imerovigli and you won't soon forget. You will be able to savor excellent delicacies there that are sure to please your palate. These meals combine the unique flavors of Santorini with a Mediterranean flair.

- **La Maison**

Are you hankering after a wonderful, romantic dinner while overlooking the stunning blue sea? If so, you should check out La Maison Restaurant in the Imerovigli hamlet on the island of Santorini! La Maison Restaurant offers a variety of dishes that are both simple and incredibly excellent, so it can cater to a wide range of tastes.

- **Mylos**

The Mylos Filippi Coffee Shop Lounge Greek Mylos Cafe is named after a windmill because it is constructed around one. During peak season, the cafeteria gets rather busy due to its stunning caldera view from the terrace, especially at night.

- **Volkan on the Rocks**

Volkan On The Rocks is a gorgeous spot in Fira with a view of the caldera, the sea, and the setting sun. Volkan On The Rocks' facilities, which include a restaurant, a cinema, a cocktail bar, a cafe, and a wine bistro, is perfect for a genuine Cycladic experience.

- **Vineyart**

To sample some of the greatest wine and culinary creations in Oia, Vineyard is a great place to visit. It's a wine bar restaurant with a large menu of locally produced wines and delicious Greek and Mediterranean fare created with premium ingredients.

- **Skaros**

Situated in front of Skaros Rock in Imerovigli, Skaros Fish Tavern offers a delightful atmosphere and breathtaking views. The catch of the day is highlighted on the menu, along with other really good dishes made with basic traditional preparations like garlic and lemon.

- **Theros wave**

Theros Wave is the best spot to unwind and spend a few hours in this idyllic location. It consists of three buildings: a restaurant, a beach bar, and a large area with lounge chairs that are perfect for unwinding and practicing meditation.

- **Feggera**

The exquisite gourmet dinners served at Feggera restaurant, which is situated on a gorgeously designed terrace, blend flavors of Santorini and Cretan cuisine. You can sample Mediterranean food at Feggera while taking in the breathtaking vista of the ancient Megalochori city.

- **To Psaraki**

The Psaraki restaurant is located a short distance from Vlychada Beach. This is the ideal location to sample authentic Greek cuisine in its purest and tastiest form. The restaurant offers a variety of cuisines.

- **Aktaion**

For more than a century, Aktaion has served opulent yet traditional cuisine focused on authentic Santorini flavors, fine local libations, and breathtaking views of the island's caldera.

## Best Time to Visit

It all depends on your goals. Would you like to travel to Santorini during the off-season when prices are lower? For the best weather, would you like to visit Santorini? When there are fewer tourists, is that when you would like to visit Santorini?

One of the island's special qualities is that it caters to a wide range of tourists, including families, couples, students, and those looking to spend a lot of money on a fancy restaurant or a private villa perched on a cliff overlooking the sunset and volcano. Accommodation options in Santorini include hostels, camping, bed and breakfasts, hotels, apartments, and villas.

The black beaches of Monolithos, Kamari, Perissa, Perivolos, and the nearby villages of Messaria and Finikia are more affordable, while the most costly places to stay in Santorini are the Cliffside and Villas and Suites with Caldera View.

The best times to find hotel deals are from March through late May (excluding Orthodox Easter), and from late September through December.

If you're willing to select from the few hotels that remain open, the winter season is the least expensive.

Purchase your tickets in advance to avoid disappointment, as availability may be limited during peak season or on holidays such as Holy Spirit Day or Orthodox Easter.

1. Be advised that many ferry boats to the islands stop traveling in the middle of October.
2. Superjets and high-speed boats stop traveling earlier

Although June through mid-September can be hot enough, **July and August are the hottest months.**

There are many activities to enjoy and Santorini is a fantastic location for nearly all types of vacation activities.

Magnificent scenery, mountains and beaches, hiking and museums showcasing rare and fascinating artifacts, delicious food accessible to all budgets, cooking classes, traditional performances, historic cave wineries, breweries, and canvas situated in the oldest vineyards in Europe, catamaran and fishing excursions, and tours of the volcanoes will keep you occupied for the duration of your visit!

Relishing in the Caldera while sipping coffee or a drink and taking in the breathtaking view of the surrounding Aspronissi, Palea Kameni, Nea Kameni, and Thirassia volcanoes is an invaluable experience. Selecting the ideal time to visit Santorini depends on your knowledge of the island's weather during the various months of the year.

The months of **April through early May and mid-September through early November** have the nicest weather.

- It's usually not too hot, which makes it simple to travel the island, see and do a lot of activities, ride a bike or go on a trek, and see the sights.
- It might rain a little at times, so you should be ready.
- You can expect fresh mornings, and cool nights but quite mild days.
- It may be windy, but less than during certain other months.
- Great time to visit Santorini if you encounter some health concerns or attempting to avoid the heat.
- These months, there's a restricted choice of restaurants and taverns operating.
- **November** is off-season for the known nightclubs and bars.
- Fira is where you'll mostly find some nighttime life.

- The ideal time of year to visit is thought to be **May and September–October** for tourists, photographers, and those seeking less oppressive heat.
- The months of **March**, **April**, and **May** are when the weather gets better, costs go down, some tourist shops open, and a lot of hotels and attractions are prepared to welcome visitors. There is usually an improvement in the weather, with crisp mornings and evenings. Although it may rain and occasionally be overcast, Santorini's spring will surprise you with an abundance of blooms and more greenery than typical following the previous winter's rainfall.
- The busiest travel months are **June** through **September** when everything is accessible. Prices are at an all-time high, so reservations should be made well in advance to guarantee a place to stay due to the strong demand. Early booking discounts are offered to those who make reservations in advance; but, due to great

demand, last-minute availability is nearly nonexistent in July and August.
- There are fewer events in **October and November** because the season is about to finish. Some stores are still open, but lodging facilities are gradually closing. Still, the weather is generally pleasant, with the calm of fall and many days without crowds. Unlike other regions of Europe (and even Northern and Central Greece), where cold weather has already come, tourists may make the most of Santorini while still enjoying the mild weather.
- The colder months of **December, January**, and **February** see fewer visitors and closed attractions.

## The Cheapest Time To Travel

Travelers typically try to stay away from crowds to have a good experience.

**August** is the peak season for crowded beaches and bad experiences in Santorini.

For travelers on a tight budget, the off-season, which spans from the end of **October to March,** is the ideal time to visit Santorini because hotels have empty rooms and airfares are less.

In **April and October,** when seasonal transportation and tour fees are less expensive, deals are also to be found.

Affordably priced lodging and pleasant weather can be found in early **May or mid-October.**

If money is tight, look for lodging options like camping, B&Bs, and hostels on the fringes of the towns. You can save money on airfare and lodging by planning your vacation well in advance.

While the weather can be difficult, you can be fortunate to get inexpensive aircraft tickets from Athens to Santorini in the winter, March–April, and October–November.

Time to enjoy calm weather, moderate light, stunning sunsets, a swim in mildly chilly seas, and meditation is right at the start of November.

For photographers, this is also the ideal time of year, along with April and a portion of May, since clear skies are necessary for quality shots.

It's rare to get a picture of one of those amazing sunsets you could hope for during the summer months because of the heat.

# CHAPTER 5

## Transportation Options

### How to Navigate Santorini

Navigate the breathtaking island of Santorini with luxury, ease, and convenience!

With its magnificent waters, charming villages, and breathtaking slopes, as well as its exciting nightlife and breathtaking sunsets, Santorini has all the makings of Greece's most popular tourist destination.

Even though Santorini is a small island, if you haven't planned, hopping from place to place might cause worry and aggravation at the last minute.

- **Rent a Vehicle**

You can travel anywhere on the island at any time and explore at your leisure when you have your mode of transportation.

Renting a car makes almost all of the best things to do in Santorini easier and more enjoyable. You won't have any risk of getting lost on the little island, so relax!

Renting a car is the greatest and possibly safest way to get to Santorini. When you arrive, rent one at the port or airport to avoid having to wait for a bus or taxi!

In Santorini, renting a car is as cheap as thirty euros a day, and you can just return it to the rental agency.

- **Rent a quad or an ATV**

Make reservations for a day's ATV/QUAD in Santorini to up the thrill factor. The rental fee starts at thirty euros per day and varies depending on the length of your reservation

For an exciting day of exploration with friends, it would be wise to schedule a ride, as the mode of transportation is prone to instability and disasters.

- **Rent a Motorbike**

Riding a motorbike is another quick and simple method to get around Santorini.

Most of them are parking-compatible everywhere and have automatic transmissions. Moreover, the daily fee starts at just twenty euros!

Before renting a car, keep the following in mind:

- The island can get quite busy with tourists, and the small roads may get crowded

- Drive carefully
- Only rent a car if you have prior driving experience
- Parking spaces can fill up rapidly, particularly in Fira Town and Oia Village.
- You should also drive on the right side of the road
- Majority of rental companies require that you have an international or European driver's license.

**Take a Bus**

All bus itineraries begin and end at Fira Town, which is home to Santorini's primary bus station.

With rates ranging from 1.8 to 2.5 euros, it's the least expensive way to get about the island, even though it won't get you everywhere.

There are set and predetermined bus stops; you cannot get off at any random location. You might have to wait for the next one if they arrive crowded with passengers.

It's also important to note that bus travel is a cash-only operation. Thus, when you get in the car, don't forget to bring spare coins.

Buses depart from Fira and stop at several well-known hotels, landmarks, and small towns

- **Itinerary for Fira to Kamari**

During the summer, the bus arrives every fifteen minutes.

Route: Mesa Gonia - Kamari - Karterados - Messaria - Koutsougianopoulos winery

- **Perissa – Fira The Express Route**

During the summer, the bus arrives every half an hour.

Route: Emporio - Perivolos - Perissa - Fira - El Greco hotel - Volcano View hotel - Santo Wines

- **Perissa – Fira Route**

In the summer, the bus arrives every 30 minutes.

Route: Fira - Karterados - Messaria - Vothonas - Pyrgos - Emporio - Megalochori - Perivolos - Perissa

- **Akrotiri – Fira Route**

The bus arrives once every 20 minutes throughout the summer.

Route: Red Beach – Akrotiri – Fira – El Greco hotel – Volcano View hotel – Santo Wines – Megalochori hamlet

- **Fira – Oia Route Plan**

In the summer, the bus arrives every 15 minutes.

Route: Imerovigli – Finikia – Oia – Fira – Firostefani

- **Itinerary for Fira -Airport**

Bus service operates every hour during the summer. Route: Messaria - Karterados - Fira - Airport

Further information regarding the bus routes is available on **KTEL** Santorini's official website.

Please be aware that there might only be one bus every hour or that certain itineraries might not be available at night. Observe that the buses on each route come at different times. When making travel plans, you will need to consult the schedule to determine their arrival and departure timings.

**Take a Taxi**

Santorini Cabs are the best option if you want a more opulent travel than using the bus!

These cars have a clean, contemporary appearance thanks to their glossy gray-silver surface.

On the flip side, there aren't many taxis operating on the roads at night during the peak season, so it could be difficult to find one.

There are a few taxi stands at the airport and Athinios port, but the only one is in Fira Town.

The taxi central bus station's number is **0030 22860-22-555**

**Make a Private Transfer Reservation**

These opulent minivans are dependable and high-quality, guaranteeing optimal comfort and convenience, even though they are marginally more costly than traditional modes of transportation.

To avoid standing in line for extended periods, needless delays, and other issues, many passengers opt to reserve private airport and port transports.

The cheerful and helpful nature of the minivan drivers in the area is another advantage. During your visit, they will gladly offer you travel advice and recommend hip locations for you to check out.

This is by far the most efficient way to go from the port or airport to your accommodation and back. It enables visitors to get the most out of their stay on the island of Santorini.

# CHAPTER 6

## Greek Phrases for Visitors

While English is widely spoken in tourist areas, locals appreciate visitors who make an effort to speak their language. key Greek phrases that will not only help you navigate Santorini with ease but also foster connections with the warm-hearted locals.

**Basic Greetings and Courtesies**

- Hello - Γεια σας (Ya sas): A versatile greeting used throughout the day. It's a friendly way to start conversations with locals.
- Goodbye - Αντίο (Adio): When parting ways, this is a polite way to bid farewell.
- Please - Παρακαλώ (Parakaló): An essential word when making requests or seeking assistance.
- Thank you - Ευχαριστώ (Efharistó): Express gratitude with this universally appreciated phrase.

- Excuse me / I'm sorry - Συγγνώμη (Signómi): Use this phrase to apologize or get someone's attention politely.

**Navigating Places and Directions**

- Where is...? - Πού είναι...; (Pou íne...?): Handy when looking for specific locations or attractions. Useful when shopping or inquiring about prices.
- Left - Αριστερά (Aristerá) / Right - Δεξιά (Dexiá): Navigate the charming streets of Santorini by asking for directions.
- Straight ahead - Κατευθείαν (Kateytheían): Useful for confirming you're on the right path.

**Dining and Culinary Phrases**

- I would like... - Θα ήθελα... (Tha íthela...): Use this phrase when ordering in restaurants or cafes.
- The check, please - Τον λογαριασμό, παρακαλώ (Ton logariasmó, parakaló): Request the bill when you're ready to settle your meal.

- Delicious - Νόστιμο (Nóstimo): Show appreciation for the delightful Greek cuisine.

**Cultural Connection Phrases**

- What is your name? - Πώς σε λένε; (Pos se léne?): Engage in friendly conversations by asking someone's name.
- Nice to meet you - Χάρηκα (Charíka): When you first meet someone, tell them how much you like them.
- Can you recommend...? - Μπορείτε να προτείνετε...; (Boríte na protínete...?): Seek recommendations for local attractions or experiences.

**Expressing Emotions**

- I love it here - Το αγαπάω εδώ (To agapáo edó): Share your admiration for Santorini's beauty:
- I am lost - Χάθηκα (Cháthika): In case you become lost, ask for assistance.

- Help! - Βοήθεια! (Voítheia!): Reach out for assistance in urgent situations.

**Numbers and Basic Shopping Phrases**

- One, Two, Three - Ένα (Éna), Δύο (Dýo), Τρία (Tría): Learn these essential numbers for basic transactions.
- How much does it cost? - Πόσο κοστίζει; (Póso kostízei?): Useful when shopping or bargaining.

**Expressions of Gratitude**

- Thank you very much - Ευχαριστώ πολύ (Efharistó polý): Convey deep appreciation with this extended thank you.
- You're welcome - Παρακαλώ (Parakaló): Respond graciously when someone expresses gratitude.

**Emergency Phrases**

- Where is the nearest hospital? - Πού είναι το πλησιέστερο νοσοκομείο; (Pou íne to plisíestro

nosokomío?): In case of emergencies, this phrase can be crucial
- Call the police - Καλέστε την αστυνομία (Kaléste tin astynomía): Use this phrase when immediate assistance is required.

**Expressing Appreciation**

- This place is stunning - Αυτό το μέρος είναι εκπληκτικό (Aftó to méros íne ekpliktikó): Convey your awe and admiration for the breathtaking beauty of Santorini.
- Your home is lovely - Το σπίτι σας είναι υπέροχο (To spíti sas íne ypérocho): If invited into someone's home, express your appreciation for their hospitality.

**Cultural Engagement**

- Tell me more about your culture - Πες μου περισσότερα για τον πολιτισμό σας (Pes mou perissótera ya ton politismó sas):

Encourage locals to share insights about their cultural heritage.

- I would love to learn Greek - Θα ήθελα να μάθω Ελληνικά (Tha íthela na mátho Elliniká): Express your interest in learning the Greek language, showcasing genuine enthusiasm for the local culture.

**Navigating Complex Interactions**

- Can you help me find my way? - Μπορείτε να με βοηθήσετε να βρω το δρόμο μου; (Boríte na me voithísete na vro to drómo mou?):
- Seek assistance for intricate navigation situations, such as finding specific locations.
- I'm lost, can you guide me? - Χάθηκα, μπορείτε να με καθοδηγήσετε; (Cháthika, boríte na me kathodigísete?): Politely ask for guidance if you find yourself disoriented in an unfamiliar area.

**Culinary Sophistication**

- Could you recommend a local delicacy? - Μπορείτε να προτείνετε μια τοπική λιχουδιά; (Boríte na protínete mia topikí lichudiá?): Explore the culinary wonders of Santorini by asking for recommendations beyond the standard menu.
- I'm a vegetarian/vegan - Είμαι χορτοφάγος/καταναλωτής φυτικών προϊόντων (Íme chortofágos/katanalotís fitikón proïónton): communicate dietary preferences to ensure a seamless dining experience.

**Connecting on a Deeper Level**

- What is the significance of this tradition? - Ποια είναι η σημασία αυτού του έθιμου; (Pia íne i simasía aftú tu éthimu?): Foster meaningful conversations by expressing curiosity about local traditions.
- Can you share a local story with me? - Μπορείτε να μοιραστείτε μαζί μου μια τοπική ιστορία;

(Boríte na mirestíte mazí mu mia topikí istoría?): Encourage storytelling to learn more about the island's history and folklore.

## Festivals And Events

An old saying states that Santorini has more wine than water and more churches than houses. Because they cherish customs and religion, Santorinians arrange religious feasts with great enthusiasm. Days before the feast day, preparations typically begin. These include preparing meals and keeping the church decorated. Every hamlet celebrates its patron saint with a variety of rituals and religious events. The ritual is particularly moving on Easter and the feast day of the Holy Virgin; residents light candles and participate in a march around Santorini's communities.

**Cultural Events**

Santorini holds fascinating cultural events in the summer.

- **Festival Ifestia**

Every August, Santorini hosts the Ifestia Festival, also known as the Greek Volcano Festival. It includes a fireworks-filled depiction of a volcano eruption along with several engaging activities, dancing shows, and concerts.

- **International Music Festival**

Musicians are invited to perform for two weeks in September in Fira as part of the International Music Festival.

- **Religion and Feast Festivals**

**Easter;**Santorini celebrates Easter with a melancholy grandeur. On Holy Friday, the ambiance in the town of Pyrgos is very mesmerizing, especially with the streets lit by candles.

**May 29:**The village of Akrotiri Agia Theodosia's feast day.

**The first of July:** The village of Megalochori celebrates Agioi Anargyroi's feast day.

**The 20th of July:** The communities of Fira and Imerovigli celebrate Prophet Ilias' feast day.

**25 July** : The village of Vothonos celebrates Agia Anni's feast day.

**July 27:** The village of Vourvoulos celebrates Agios Panteleimon's feast day.

**August 4th:** Finikia village celebrates the feast day of the Holy Seven Children.

**August 6th:** The communities of Pyrgos, Akrotiri, and Fira celebrate the feast day of the Transfiguration of Christ.

**August 15th:** Akrotiri, Firostefani, and the majority of Santorini's villages mark the Diocese of the Virgin Mary's feast day. The church of Panagia Episkopi hosts the largest festivity in Santorini on the feast day of the Holy Virgin.

The day before, traditional cuisine and regional wine are served to the attendees as part of the preparations.

**August 29th:** The town of Monolithos celebrates Agios Ioannis' feast day.

**August 31st;** In Kamari village, people celebrate Agia Zoni's feast day.

**September 14th:** Holy Cross Feast Day, observed in the Holy Cross Church in Perissa Village.

**September 20:** Kontohori village celebrates Agios Efstathios' feast day

**September 24:** Kamari village celebrates Mary Myrtidiotissa's feast day

 **The 20th of October:** The village of Firostefani celebrates Agios Gerasimos' feast day

**October 22nd:** The village of Emporio celebrates the feast day of Agios Averkios, the patron saint of wine.

**26 October:** The village of Messaria celebrates Agios Dimitrios' feast day.

**1st November**: The village of Messaria celebrates Agioi Anargyroi's feast day.

**November 11:** Agios Minas' feast day, which is observed in the Agios Minas church in Fira village.

**December 6th:** The Monastery of Agios Nikolaos in Thira village celebrates the feast day of Agios Nikolaos.

**December 9th:** The village of Vothonos celebrates Agia Anni's feast day

**December 12th:** Pyrgos, Emporio, and Oia villages celebrate Agios Spyridon's feast day

**December 13th:** The village of Vourvoulos celebrates Agios Efstratios' feast day

**December 15th:** Kontohori village celebrates Agios Eleftherios' feast day

# CHAPTER 7

## Cuisines To Try

Deeply influenced by Greek customs, the island's food is a tasteful fusion of seasonal ingredients, Mediterranean flavors, and distinctive regional delicacies. Each meal serves as a call to taste the very best of this charming island.

## Traditional Santorinian Cuisine

Santorini's traditional meals, which individually tell a tale of the island's rich history and cultural influences, are the essence of the island's gastronomic identity.

- Santorinis Fava

Fava Santorinis, a creamy yellow split pea purée, is a great place to start your culinary journey. Its earthy taste and silky texture make it a great prelude to a Santorinian feast, whether served as a side dish or dip.

- Tomatokeftedes

Santorini's volcanic soil is ideal for growing tomatoes, which results in the creation of tomato fritters seasoned with herbs and spices. These crispy snacks are a lovely way to highlight the fresh vegetables from the island.

- Melitzanosalata

This smokey eggplant dip provides a taste explosion of Mediterranean cuisine. It's a classic appetizer that perfectly encapsulates the essence of Santorini's sun-kissed ingredients when served with warm bread.

- Moussaka

Tuck into this filling baked meal that consists of layers of eggplant, minced beef, and béchamel sauce. A hearty dish that embodies the Greeks' passion for complex, multi-layered flavors.

- Souvlaki

Without souvlaki, no investigation of Greek food is complete.

It is a popular street snack that perfectly captures the flavor and simplicity of Greek cuisine, whether it be skewered meat or vegetables that have been grilled and perfectly seasoned.

- The Sea's Bounty

Delectable Fresh Seafood, Santorini's abundance of fresh seafood, along with its charming coastline setting, creates a symphony of flavors that reflects the island's marine past.

- Grilled Octopus

Savor this Santorini specialty, Grilled Octopus. Perfectly cooked and blackened, this fish dish is sometimes topped with herbs and drizzled with olive oil, demonstrating the island's expertise in seafood preparation.

- Astakomakaronada

The star of upmarket seafood restaurants is Astakomakaronada, a sumptuous lobster pasta. Enjoy the perfect combination of al dente pasta and juicy lobster.

- Psarosoupa

The island's close ties to the sea are reflected in this traditional fisherman's soup. Packed full of the day's catch, it's a tasty homage to Santorini's fishing history.

- Vineyard Bounty

Special Wines with a View, The extraordinary wines of Santorini are a result of the volcanic soil and distinctive grape varietals. It would be impossible to visit this island's wineries and vineyard settings without taking a food tour.

- Assyrtiko Wine

Santorini is home to the world-famous crisp white wine, Assyrtiko. It is a pleasant accompaniment to seafood dishes, adding to the overall eating experience with its lemony flavors and mineral undertones.

- Vinsanto

Finish your dinner with this sweet wine made from sun-dried grapes.

Its deep, caramelized tastes, developed over time in oak barrels, make it the ideal way to cap up your Santorini culinary exploration.

- Assorted Mezedes

Small dishes served as appetizers, showcasing various flavors.

- Sun-Dried Tomatoes

Intensely flavored tomatoes, preserved under the sun.

- Kopania

Marinated olives, a staple of Greek dining.

- Ladenia

Olive oil flatbread topped with tomatoes, onions, and herbs.

- Kavourmas

Preserved meat, often pork, seasoned with spices.

- Pomegranate Loukoum

Sweet confection infused with pomegranate flavor.

- Koulouri

Circular bread rings, often sprinkled with sesame seeds.

- Thyme Honey

Local honey with distinct thyme flavors.

- Village Salads

Fresh salads with tomatoes, cucumbers, olives, and feta.

- Santorini Capers

Briny capers are grown in volcanic soil.

- Santorini Oregano

Fragrant oregano with unique volcanic terroir.

- Chloro Cheese

Local cheese with a distinct taste from Apano Meria.

- Krasotyri Cheese

Semi-hard cheese with a wine-soaked rind.

- Xynotyro Cheese

Tangy cheese made from goat or sheep milk.

- Bougatsa

Flaky pastry filled with sweet or savory fillings.

- Kakavia

Fisherman's soup with a variety of seafood.

- Rakomelo

Traditional drink combining raki, honey, and spices.

- Lamb Kleftiko

Slow-cooked lamb, marinated with herbs and spices.

- Santorini Cherry Tomatoes

Small, sweet tomatoes grown in volcanic soil.

- Pistachio Delights

Desserts featuring locally grown pistachios.

## Gourmet Experiences

For those looking for a sophisticated dining experience, Santorini is home to chic restaurants that creatively and deftly reinterpret Greek food.

- Selene Restaurant in Pyrgos

Located in the center of Pyrgos, Selene is a gastronomic landmark renowned for its creative interpretation of Santorinian cuisine. Savor a culinary adventure with carefully prepared dishes that highlight regional cuisines.

- Lauda Restaurant in Oia

Located atop the cliffs in Oia, Lauda provides elegant dining beside a picturesque outlook. A refuge for foodies, it features inventive Mediterranean dishes, a beautiful environment, and great service.

## Events & Culinary Festivals

Honoring the Flavors of Santorini

Santorini is home to several food-related events that honor the island's culinary legacy and encourage tourists to interact with regional farmers and chefs.

- Santorini Gastronomy Days

Every year, this event highlights the island's delectable cuisine. To further explore Santorini's culinary culture, local chefs host events, tastings, and courses.

- Wine Tasting Tours

Visit Santorini's cellars and vineyards by going on a wine-tasting tour. Talk to producers, discover how wine is made, and enjoy fine wines with regional specialties.

- Visit the wonderful Sikinos Bakery in Emporio

As you venture into the neighborhood. Using ancient recipes, this hidden gem creates classic Greek sweets like Bougatsa and Melitinia.

Savor delectable layers and sweet fillings that will take you back to the origins of Greek cuisine.

- Pyrgos's Local Honey

Despite its medieval appeal, Pyrgos has a hidden secret: local honey. Discover the unique aromas of thyme and wildflower honey, which are a monument to the island's rich flora, by visiting one of the honey farms tucked away in the town.

- Panigyria Celebrations in Megalochori

Immerse yourself in the heart of Santorinian culture by attending the Panigyria celebrations in Megalochori. These customary celebrations offer not only a spiritual feast but also a culinary extravaganza, showcasing regional specialties and handcrafted sweets.

- Tsipouro Tasting in Akrotiri

In addition to its many archaeological treasures, Akrotiri is home to a lively secret: Tsipouro. Sample this traditional Greek spirit in local tavernas and enjoy a taste of authentic island conviviality with mezedes (small dishes) to go with it.

- Koulouria Bakery in Fira

Nestled in Fira, Koulouria Bakery tempts with its assortment of Koulouri – circular bread rings often sprinkled with sesame seeds. As you stroll through the quaint streets of Kamari, the island's capital, these delicious baked delicacies provide a filling snack.

- Asyrtiko Gelato in Kamari

Kamari's black sand beach is not only a picturesque retreat but also a distinct flavor of nirvana. Savor Asyrtiko Gelato, a regional take on the traditional ice cream that has been blended with the crisp flavors of Asyrtiko, the white wine that is emblematic of Santorini.

- Pomegranate pleasures in Finikia

Discover the charm of pomegranate pleasures in Finikia, a sleepy village close to Oia. Try some of the region's sweet treats, such as pomegranate syrup and pomegranate loukoum, to get a taste of this ruby-red fruit that is considered auspicious and prosperous.

- Exo Gonia Village Tavernas

Nestled away from the busy crowds, Exo Gonia hides real village tavernas where residents congregate. Take in the warmth of Greek hospitality while enjoying food that has been lovingly prepared using traditional methods.

- Local Cheeses in Apano Meria

Artisanal cheese makers can be found in Apano Meria, the less visited northern region of Santorini. Savor the deep flavors of regional cheeses such as Xynotyro, Krasotyri, and Chloro, which individually capture the unique terroir of Santorini.

- Tholos Cherry Tomatoes

Tholos is a peaceful community close to Fira that is well-known for its cherry tomatoes. Explore nearby fields to sample these tiny, delectable gems, which are frequently sun-dried to enhance their flavor and provide a genuine taste of Santorini's agricultural expertise.

- Rakomelo in Imerovigli

Ascend the charming pathways of Imerovigli and experience the coziness of Rakomelo. This traditional beverage offers a warm respite while you take in the expansive views. It is made by blending raki, a spirit made from grapes, with honey and spices.

- Local Bakeries in Messaria

The modest charm of Messaria also permeates its neighborhood bakeries. Indulge in the simple joys of Santorini life by making Greek coffee and freshly baked pastries like Bougatsa and Koulouri your daily ritual.

## Well-known Cafes

**To Kafenedaki tou Emboriou**

- Opening Time: 10:00 AM to 8:00 PM
- Cuisines: Greek, Mediterranean, and café

- Special Diets: Suitable for vegetarians
- Meals: Breakfast

**The lounge bar Iriana Cafe**

- Opening Time: 9:00 AM - 12:00 AM
- Cuisines: Greek, Mediterranean, and European
- Special Diets: Vegan and Vegetarian-Friendly Selections
- Meals: Brunch, Late Night, Dinner, Lunch, and Drinks

**Akrothiri Eat Drink and Heal Bistro**

- Opening time: 7:30 AM to 12:00 AM
- Cuisines: Greek, Mediterranean, and café
- Special Diets: Gluten-free, vegan, and vegetarian options

Still, they were possibly the most delicious pancakes I have ever tasted.

**Rooftop View of KooKoo Bar Restaurant**

- Opening time: 8:00 AM - 6:00 PM

- Cuisines: Greek, Healthy, Bar, Café, Dining Bars
- Special Diets: Vegan and Vegetarian-Friendly Selections

Great location, but closes early for Dinner

**Galini Cafe**

- Opening time 8:00 AM to 11:00 PM
- Cuisines: Greek, Mediterranean and Café
- Special Diets: Gluten-free, vegan, and vegetarian options
- Meals: Brunch, Lunch, Breakfast, and Drinks

**JuiceMe**

- Opening Time: 8:00 AM to 11:00 PM
- Cuisines: Healthy, Mediterranean, Café
- Special Diets: Gluten-free, vegan, and vegetarian options
- Meals: Brunch, Breakfast

**Tutti Frutti**

- Opening time: 9:00 AM to 10:00 PM

- Cuisines: Greek, Mediterranean, Fast Food, and Healthy
- Special Diets: Gluten-free, vegan, and vegetarian options

**The Finch**

- Opening time: 8:30 AM to 11:45 PM
- Cuisines: European, bar, cafe, and dining bars
- Special Diets: Vegan and Vegetarian-Friendly Options

**Brusco Wine and Coffee Deli**

- Opening time: 12:00 AM to 11:59 PM
- Cuisines: Greek, Wine Bar, Cafe
- Special Diets: Gluten-free, vegan, and vegetarian options
- Meals: Breakfast, Lunch, Dinner, and Brunch

**Chocolate Creperie Cafe**

- Opening time: 11:00 AM to 11:00 PM
- Cuisines: Café, Continental

- Special Diets: Suitable for vegetarians

**Coffee Lab**

- Opening time: 6:00 AM to 9:00 PM
- Cuisines: Café
- Special Diets: Suitable for vegetarians
- Meals: Brunch, Breakfast

**Terra Nera**

- Opening time: 8:00 AM to 11:00 PM
- Cuisines: Mediterranean, European, Grill, Pizza, and Café
- Special Diets: Gluten-free, vegan, and vegetarian options

**Santo Fresh**

- Opening time: 12:00 AM to 11:59 PM
- Cuisines: Greece's cafe
- Special Diets: Plant-Based Choices
- Meals: Breakfast

**The Hungry Donkey**

- Opening time: 12:00 AM to 11:59 PM
- Cuisines: Café, Continental
- Special Diets: Vegan and Vegetarian-Friendly Selections
- Meals: Drinks, Late Night, Brunch, Lunch, and Breakfast

**Melenio**

- Opening time: 12:00 AM to 11:59 PM
- Cuisines: Greece's cafe
- Meals: Drinks, Late Night, and Breakfast

# CHAPTER 8

## Shopping in Santorini

### Top Shopping Destinations

### What to Buy and Where to Shop?

Santorini's main draw is its shopping, which features everything from stylish antiques to the newest in haute couture clothes, as well as lively traditional markets selling fruits and vegetables. You can stroll through neighborhoods lining huge department stores, independent boutiques, art galleries, and souvenir shops brimming with locally manufactured ceramics. You can even peruse bookshops brimming with rare and best-selling titles.

You could spend weeks shopping in Santorini. This vibrant Greek island can be visited solely for the sake of shopping. See what to buy by visiting some of Santorini's top shopping destinations.

## Fira

Dress elegantly, and adorn yourself.

Santorini's city, Fira, is a major shopping destination with an enormous assortment of stores selling a wide range of goods, including jewelry, clothing, and housewares. The well-known "Gold Street" in the city center is home to over 40 jewelers that offer chains, gold, silver, precious and semiprecious stones, and other adornments. While some of these stores have ultramodern displays, many provide handcrafted, genuine goods that are genuinely one-of-a-kind and steeped in island tradition. Additionally, stores selling bags and accessories along with the newest styles in Greek haute fashion can be found in the city center. Fira is the place to go if you want to outfit yourself with elegance.

## Santorini Ceramic & Pottery Shops

Acquire some tasteful, one-of-a-kind plates and pots. You may get incredibly lovely,

Handcrafted souvenirs and gifts in Santorini's ceramic and pottery boutiques, which will make a statement piece for your home decor. You will be mesmerized and astounded by the exquisitely made bowls, plates, cups, pitchers, pots, vases, and various ceramics and pottery. Here, there are a lot of pottery shops that meticulously make everything they sell by hand with love. The intricate decorations and shaping are stunning. They can also create unique pottery to fulfill specific requests. Replica, a well-known pottery and ceramics store in Oia, is one of the best in Santorini. Almost every town and village has wonderful ceramics and pottery stores.

**Hondos Center Santorini**

A large department store, Hondos Center Santorini has everything you might need, including toys, apparel, toiletries, and style for all. It is well-known for carrying a wide range of high-end, name-brand cosmetics from producers including Clinique, Lancôme, Christian Dior, and Estée Lauder.

Professional beauticians are available to offer advice and suggestions on the ideal hues and looks for you. In addition to clothing, beachwear, shoes, purses, and hair and body care products, these stores also sell fashion.

You may get anything for the youngsters, including plush animals, action figures, and other toys. Hondos Center is situated in a crowded pedestrian zone with cobblestones in the center of Fira.

**Santorini Art Galleries**

Examine everything, including sculptures and wall art.

Every kind of cultural expression is available at Santorini's art galleries, including paintings, sculptures, bas-reliefs, tapestries, and other wall and decorative arts in addition to handcrafted jewelry. Beautiful galleries brimming with elaborate paintings can be seen, and the original pieces created by the artists themselves are for sale. Some are located in lovely ancient basements and wine cellars, while others are in brightly lit,

Ultramodern galleries with stark white walls. Others display amazing sculptures and handcrafted goods that can be purchased.

There is an incredible amount of beautiful art. AK Art Foundation and 2U Santorini in Fira, Art Space in Exo Gonia, Epilekton and Galanopoulos in Oia, and Hand-Crafted Workshop in Kamari are a few of the well-known Santorini galleries.

**Epilekton**

Discover a world full of undiscovered gems.

From handmade pottery, sculptures, paintings, and antique bells to a breathtaking collection of varied folk art and collectible items gathered from all over the world, Epilekton has it all. This 1920-founded location in the center of Oia offers a broad selection of the strange, lovely, and bizarre, so you may find a genuinely one-of-a-kind present or souvenir to remember your trip. Vintage maps, coin collections, postcards, comic books, and a variety of uncommon finds and trinkets are all available here. You can unearth secret treasures there that you never would have imagined.

**The Fruit Markets**

Santorini Fruit markets is a particular kind of traditional farmers' market; they open early in the evening and sell freshly gathered fruits from all over the island. These locations are the epitome of romanticism, with their lovely scents and the soothing sound of the waves lapping against the shoreline, somewhere between a produce market and a night market. Here's your chance to experience the greatest fruit you've ever tasted, soak in local culture, and have a unique retreat after a day of meandering through villages or lazing on beaches. The Oia fruit market, which offers fantastic produce just inches from the seaside, is one of the most well-liked fruit markets.

**Fabrica Shopping Center**

Offering the largest name brands in a deeply historic setting, Fabrica Shopping Center is an outdoor mall housed in a former historic flour mill. Spread on three levels, this location provides visitors with the pinnacle of shopping and entertainment under azure sky, while also providing breathtaking views of the island's picturesque volcano. Along with well-known brands like Fila, Galatis, Pink Woman, and Adidas, this mall also houses restaurants like Ouzeri Fabrica Greek Food and Espresso Café. Additionally, the Mati Art Gallery, Mavrolithos Souvenir Shop, and Pili Hand Made Accessories all sell handmade arts and crafts. Among the biggest, this was the island's first commercial center. It is located in Fira's center.

**The Nomikos Street**

Located in the center of the Oia neighborhood, Nomikos Street is a major thoroughfare that caters to boutique, antique, and commercial shoppers. It houses nearly all types of independent and well-known stores in one location. It is a bustling location that is well-liked by both locals and tourists. It also boasts amazing sunsets and serves as a gateway to some of Oia's most popular vistas. You can find a lot of gems here, whether you're searching for the newest trends in fashion, handcrafted items, presents, mementos, or antiques and collectibles. Additionally, you can pause for a bite at eateries and cafés with breathtaking views of the sea. You may spend hours getting lost on this cozy, stone-paved street that is great for pedestrians.

**Atlantis Books E.E.**

Packed with rare and unusual books as well as the newest bestsellers, Atlantis Books is one of the most charming, cozy, and inviting bookstores in the Mediterranean. A group of young American and European bibliophiles founded the store to provide a haven and escape for all kinds of readers and authors. It has been creating rankings of the world's greatest bookstores regularly since 2004. It's in the center of the town of Oia, in the basement of an old-fashioned whitewashed house. Everything is available here, including comic books, nonfiction, biographies, and novels. This can be the place to find a rare gem or first edition if you're hunting for one.

# CHAPTER 9

## 5-day Trip Itinerary

### DAY 1: Discovering Santorini's Magnificence

**Morning.** Enjoy a delectable breakfast at the quaint Fira Kalamia to start your day. After that, take a beautiful trek along the Fira-Oia trek to see the famous blue-domed churches and the Aegean Sea.

**Afternoon.** Savor a delicious midday meal at Metaxy Mas, a classic Greek tavern renowned for its genuine flavors. After that, take a tour of the ancient city of Ancient Thera, which is positioned atop a hill, and become fully immersed in Santorini's rich past.

**Evening.** After a delicious dinner at Naoussa Restaurant, take in the captivating Oia sunset. After that, have a stroll around Oia's quaint streets while taking in the stunning white-washed architecture.

## DAY 2: Leisure and Island Exploration

**Morning.** Take a guided excursion to see the Santorini Volcano at the beginning of your day. Discover the volcanic islands and take in the striking scenery. After that, take a plunge in the Santorini Hot Springs to refresh yourself.

**Afternoon.** Ouzeri is a small restaurant that serves delicious lunches and is well-known for its fresh seafood. After that, spend a leisurely afternoon by the glistening seas at the gorgeous Red Beach and White Beach.

**Evening.** Savor a remarkable meal at Koukoumavlos, a well-known eatery that combines Mediterranean and Greek cuisines. Visit the White Door Theater (White Door Theatro) for a captivating cultural show to round off the evening.

DAY 3: Tasting of Wine and Cultural Delights

**Morning.** Take a morning stroll around the well-preserved Minoan Bronze Age settlement of Akrotiri. After that, savor a delicious brunch at 1800 while taking in expansive island vistas.

**Afternoon.** Taste the famous wines of Santorini by taking a guided wine-tasting tour at Artemis Karamolegos Winery. Visit Pyrgos (Pyrgos Kallistis), a lovely village with classic architecture and charming streets, afterward.

**Evening.** Savor a romantic supper at Selene Restaurant, renowned for its exquisite Greek food and sophisticated setting. Enjoy a nightcap at Katharos Lounge, a welcoming lounge with breathtaking views of the Caldera, thereafter.

DAY 4: Island Exploration and Leisure

**Morning.** Enjoy a light breakfast at La Maison, a quaint café renowned for its mouthwatering pastries, to start your day. Take a catamaran trip after that to discover Santorini's hidden treasures, which will include a stop at the Santorini Volcanic Islands trip with a Hot Springs Visit.

**Afternoon.** Santorini Premium Catamaran Cruise with Fresh BBQ & Drinks: Savor a delicious BBQ lunch and cool beverages on board the catamaran. After that, visit Perivolos Beach to enjoy the sun and swim in the crystal-clear seas.

**Evening**. Volkan on the Rocks is a restaurant that offers a unique dining experience with meals cooked using volcanic heat. Enjoy a delicious evening there. Visit Skaros Rock, a breathtaking cliffside location with expansive views of the island, to cap out the day.

## DAY 5: Farewell

**Morning.** Aigaio is a charming café overlooking the Aegean Sea. There, have a leisurely breakfast to start your day. After that, pay a visit to the serene Monastery of Profitis Ilias (Moni Profitou Iliou). It is located on the tallest mountain in Santorini.

**Afternoon.** Savor a mouthwatering lunch at Ammoudi Fish Tavern, a beachfront eatery renowned for its fish specialties. After that, take a boat to the adjacent island of Thirasia, sometimes known as Therasia, and discover its breathtaking scenery and traditional communities.

**Evening.** Savor a goodbye supper at Selene Restaurant, renowned for its elegant Greek cooking and welcoming atmosphere. Attend the fascinating cultural event with traditional Greek wedding rituals, Santorini The Greek Wedding Show Entry Tickets, to top off your trip on a high note.

# CHAPTER 10

## Traveling With Family or as a Couple

### Santorini as a Couple

It's a mystical island that makes falling in love with the island and the person you're going with quite simple! When all you can see are towering cliffs, whitewashed structures, and blue-domed cathedrals, it's impossible to not enjoy yourself. Allow the cool sea breeze to caress your hair while the sun shines down on your face and the sight of pristine, blue waters fills your heart with peace.

**Distinctive Geomorphology and Landscape**

One of the world's most romantic locations, Santorini was created thousands of years ago by a powerful volcanic eruption. It provides visitors with a singular fusion of modern architecture, scenic beauty, and historical richness.

This location is ideal for a vacation with a special someone because of its unique, natural beauty. You can make lifetime memories worth millions of dollars by exploring the stunning Caldera, volcanic beaches, and lunar vistas.

**Ideal Location for a Marriage Proposal**

There are plenty of ideal locations in Santorini for you to pop the question to your soul mate.

How about you pop the question to your loved one while the beautiful sunset is still lingering, on one knee?

**Oia** is a great place for this, but at the peak of the season, it may get very busy. An excellent substitute location for a marriage proposal is the Akrotiri Lighthouse, which provides a serene and lovely atmosphere for a proposal as the sun sets over the ocean. For a distinctive and opulent experience with their significant other, most tourists reserve a private cruise. The personnel are exceedingly helpful, competent, and kind.

**Strolls on the Romantic side and candid shots in Picturesque Villages**

There's nothing better than strolling hand in hand through a charming Santorini village with your loved one. Take photos of each other while exploring Oia and Pyrgos villages to add even more distinctive touches to your trip!

**Get Adventurous**

You're invited to spend lots of enjoyable time with your loved one on Santorini Island. Enjoy a thrilling experience by going on a catamaran trip, parasailing, scuba diving, jet skiing, or horseback riding on the beach.

**Savor Your Time in an Elegant Hotel**

In Santorini, it's easy to discover opulent hotels with welcoming personnel. A luxurious hotel perched above the Caldera cliffs, complete with a Jacuzzi and an infinity pool, will awaken your senses and make your trip the most romantic getaway you've ever had!

## Best Location for Couples

Consider booking a hotel in Pyrgos or Caldera if you're traveling with a loved one. These hotels promise to treat you like royalty and exude comfort and elegance! Additionally, they offer the same luxurious treatment at a lower cost as hotels on Caldera. Therefore, if a hotel in Caldera is out of your price range, you may still get the same royal experience by booking one in Pyrgos Village!

## Top Activities for Couples

**Reserve a Private Cruise**

Want to get the most out of your romantic getaway to Santorini with your loved one? Remember to reserve a private yacht or catamaran trip if you want to add even more special touches to your proposal. To make sure the ambiance is as romantic as possible, pick a tour that departs around sunset.

**Enjoy Your Preferred Activities**

Numerous water sports activities are available for adventure seekers. You and your spouse will enjoy taking a jet ski safari around the renowned volcano. Additionally, you can explore the entire island from the top by parasailing. You and your spouse can swim away all of your stress and exhaustion at Eros Beach. You may also enjoy the exhilaration of riding an ATV cycle with your loved one.

**Savor a Delectable Dinner**

A person's gut is the quickest route to their heart! Remember to have a special supper with your loved one at a Caldera restaurant or a fish tavern in Ammoudi.

**Go to the Monastery of Prophet Elias**

A must-see location if you and your loved one enjoy history is the Prophet Elias Monastery! With breath-taking views of the entire Santorini Islands, this lofty edifice

# Family-Friendly Activities

**Taking a caldera boat tour** is one of the things to do in Santorini with kids. The volcanic crater that houses Santorini offers a plethora of choices for exploration. This was a great way to start our vacation, and the kids loved swimming at the hot springs, exploring the stunning town of Oia, and ascending the volcano (which requires them to either hike or ride in a pack).

**Don't follow the beaten route**

Santorini caters largely to honeymooning couples. Most accommodations in Santorini were rather pricey while attempting to plan where to stay with relatives. At the center of the island, at Karterados, we slept in a family-run pension home. It felt much more local and away from the masses, even though it was only a short walk to the village of Thira and easily accessible by taxi to the rest of the island. We had a large room with a pool on the property, easy access to grocery stores (with a fridge in our room), and a sense of being able to interact with some of the locals,

Which made it an excellent place to stay with kids. While it wasn't very opulent, it was tidy and pleasant, and we had a great time visiting.

**Ride the Cable Car**

After we worked out where we were headed, the cable car stop, which connects the port with the town of Thira, was approximately a fifteen-minute walk from our hotel. The kids and I thoroughly enjoyed the breathtaking vistas. During your family vacation in Greece, taking a cable car ride is a terrific way to break up all the beach time.

**Take a family swim in Santorini's Amoudi Bay**

This is a charming, secluded little area close to Oia, yet far from the main traffic. There are many smooth, attractive pebbles to view, play with, and throw, and the waters are crystal clear, serene, and pleasant. This is a great spot for water play if you're traveling to Santorini with a little child. In other words, if your children are like mine, they will adore it.

**Visit the Beach**

Naturally. However, not all of Santorini's beaches are kid-friendly. Many of them are steep, hot, and rocky. But we also went to Monolithos, which was incredibly fun. Our top pick for a family-friendly beach in Santorini was Monolithos. Even though opinions on cleanliness vary depending on the season, it was spotless when we visited and had beach chairs, umbrellas, and showers. The warm, shallow water was immaculate, and the black sand was surprisingly smooth in this large beach area. There were a lot of Greek children present. We regarded it as a positive omen that we might have been the only native English speakers present that day.

**Watch the Sunset**

It is impossible to visit Santorini and miss the sunset. When traveling with children, witnessing the sunset can be a little challenging. Thankfully, you can easily and beautifully view it from wherever. It's convenient because you won't have to deal with the Oia throng all the time.

**Climb all 600+ steps to Thira**

Walking in the opposite direction is surprisingly enjoyable if you've already ridden the cable car in one direction. We went up, although it would have been easier for you to go down. It's pleasant to have the opportunity to stop and take in the (beautiful) surroundings, and children seem to find stairs far more entertaining than adults do. Just don't take the donkeys, as they are often mistreated horribly.

**Take a stroll or a hike**

There are many possibilities to take in stunning vistas or simply stroll around quaint little settlements on Santorini. Youngsters will enjoy running from one cobblestone to another. One of our favorite things to do when traveling with kids is to spend time outside in the great outdoors.

**Take a look at the old Thira ruins.**

It's always entertaining to stroll around and engage in archaic games. And there's lots of time to accomplish this when on a family vacation in Greece with kids!

**Get familiar with volcanoes**

There's no better place to teach a little about volcanic activity than Santorini. It was too soon to be traveling with a toddler who was just 23 months old at the time. Even though our preschooler was not yet 4 years old, he was captivated by the workings of everything and even remembered small details years later.

**Have a casual dinner with Kids**

Greek food was very popular with our kids, as I believe it would be with most youngsters. When dining with children in Greece, they enjoyed the cheese and pastries along with the crisp and fresh tomatoes and cucumbers. And a ton of Greek yogurt that is FULL fat. There was little enticing to eat, yet there was plenty to appreciate.

It seemed calm and new. A constant triumph when taking children on vacation.

# CHAPTER 11

## Emergency Contacts

These are the most helpful phone numbers that visitors to Santorini may require.

General

- Health Center (Fira) +30 22863 60300
- Municipality of Thira +30 22860 28097
- Santorini Airport +30 22860 28400
- General Telephone Area Code +30 22860
- Taxi +30 22860 22555
- Bus Service +30 22860 25404
- National Bank (Fira) +30 22860 22370
- Agrotiki Bank (Fira) +30 22860 22261
- Eurobank +30 22860 25851
- Police Station (Fira) +30 22860 22649
- Port Authority +30 22860 22239
- Post Office (Fira) +30 22860 22238
- Tourist Office (GNTO) +30 22860 27199

- Tourist Police +30 22860 22239

Other Phones

- The Museum of Musical Instruments (Oia) +30 22860 72000
- Museum of Prehistoric Thera +30 22860 23217
- Naval Museum (Oia) +30 22860 71156
- Archaeological Museum (Fira) +30 22860 22217

# CONCLUSION

I'm honored and thrilled by the adventure we've taken together as the pages of my Santorini travel guide come to an end. Travelers' hearts are forever changed by each chapter that reveals a new aspect of this Greek paradise, from the sun-kissed beaches of Perissa to the enchanted lanes of Oia.

Santorini is more than just a travel destination, with its recognizable whitewashed buildings tumbling down the cliffs, it's a tapestry of experiences stitched with threads of history, culture, and unmatched beauty. Our investigation has not only skimmed the surface but also penetrated deep into this volcanic gem's soul, unearthing hidden treasures, delectable cuisine, and subtle cultural distinctions that make Santorini an unparalleled treasure.

As our voyage comes to an end, let's take time to appreciate the beauty of Santorini's sunsets—those ethereal works of art that captivate everyone who sees them.

Santorini has painted its story on the canvas of our memories just as the sun sets, illuminating the caldera in tones of amber, pink, and gold. A story that goes beyond simple travel has been carved by every turn in the winding alleyways, every taste of Assyrtiko wine, and the rhythmic crash of waves onto the black sand beaches.

I am truly grateful to everyone who has used these words as a compass while they have been lost. Being your guide has been an honor, as I have told stories that invite you to discover, taste, and enjoy the special moments that make Santorini special. As the writer Friedrich, I understand that this guide is more than simply a list of facts; it's a key to opening doors to real experiences and revealing the essence of the island.

With its seductive fusion of contemporary charm and antiquated mythology, Santorini calls us to become more than just visitors—rather, it asks us to become actors in its continuous story. Santorini welcomes you to join its ongoing narrative, whether you are drawn to the historic remains of Akrotiri or the expansive vistas from Skaros Rock.

May the essence of Santorini stay with you when you close this guidebook and bring its essence with you on your future travels. May the memories made in the backdrop of Santorini's sunsets and seascapes endure as a testament to the life-changing potential of travel, whether you decide to revisit this island paradise or venture elsewhere.

Ultimately, Santorini is more than simply a location on a map; it's an emotion and a sensation that has no bounds in terms of time or place. I hope that your adventures will be as infinite as the Aegean horizon and as colorful as a Santorini sunset till we cross paths again on the shores of discovery. I hope your trips remain safe and that your experiences keep coming to life like the pages of an engrossing travel narrative.

Printed in Great Britain
by Amazon